Rebirth of a Sage

By: Lani Gonzales

Copyright © 2022 by Lani Gonzales

All rights reserved. Printed in the United States of America. No part of this book may be used or reproduced in any manner whatsoever without written permission except in the case of brief quotations embodied in critical articles or reviews.

The events in this book were made possible by Psycho Travels in Colombia. For more information, please visit psychotravels.co.

Front Cover Image By: @aicharactersart

ISBN: 9798356029165

First Edition: October 2022

Author's Biography

Born in the Philippines, Lani Gonzales immigrated to Virginia, USA, with her family when she was only two years old. Determined to emulate her parents' discipline and ambition, Lani worked through college and law school and is now a practicing partner in a successful law firm in Tampa, Florida. A world-traveling, volunteering, energy-healing, aspiring hypnotherapist, Lani is committed to using her light as a beacon to help others find theirs.

Dedication

To: Lauren
My Unconditional Love

To: Erza
My Joyful Love

To: Sheila, Donna, Dave, Julie, Michelle and Christina
The Lights Who Guide the Way through the Darkness

To: My Families, Chavez and Gonzales
The Shoulders on Which I Stand

To: Emilse
The Healer of Hearts

To: John Jairo
My Friend from Medellín

Contents

Author's Biography	iii
Dedication	iv
Contents	v
Introduction	1
Chapter 1 The Purge	2
Chapter 2 Love and Light	12
Chapter 3 Mothers' Wisdom	16
Chapter 4 Death	19
Chapter 5 Rebirth	27
Chapter 6 Masters	32
Chapter 7 The Comedian	35
Chapter 8 Align Hope Giver	37
Chapter 9 Integration	40
Chapter 10 The Protector of Mankind	45
Chapter 11 As Above, So Below	49

Introduction

I shit on myself. I vomited on myself.
I drooled. I spat. I howled. I cried. I screamed.
This was my journey through ayahuasca.

Like the branches of a tree and the vines of a plant, our paths twist and turn in many directions, but each branch and each vine ultimately move and grow toward the light.

My path to the light, to liberation, called me to ayahuasca. But this story is not about ayahuasca. This story, my story, is about love and light.

Chapter 1
The Purge

I was born with dark almond eyes. On the playground, children would squint their eyes attempting to mock me. A boy in middle school joked that I could be blindfolded with dental floss. At a high school football game, my friends suddenly realized that my eyes were so dark that they couldn't see my pupils. They took turns staring into my eyes, attempting to find any trace of the dark, distinguishable center. They concluded that my eyes were black and demonic.

I was reminded of my hatred for my dark, slanted Filipina eyes on a trip to Colombia to celebrate my thirty-fifth birthday with my dearest friend, Lauren. After sand blew into our eyes during an ATV ride through the mountainside of Guarne, we asked ourselves why we still wore contacts instead of getting laser eye surgery. "Is it because you're afraid?" Lauren asked. The truth: I didn't want surgery because I would no longer have a legitimate excuse to wear brown contact lenses to lighten my eyes.

After exploring the ins and outs of Medellín for four days, Lauren returned home to Florida. As for me, I stayed in Colombia to take a dark, twisted path to bring me home. *Home.*

On August 13, 2022, two days before my thirty-fifth birthday, a driver picked me up from Medellín. He was born and raised in

Medellín. He spoke very little English, and I spoke very little Spanish. After getting the "¿De donde eres?" the "Soy abogada," and other pleasantries out of the way, my driver cut to the chase.

"My name is John Jairo. I friend. I friend you." I nodded.

"¿Entiende? You understand?"

I nodded. "Sí."

We continued our drive and our efforts to make conversation despite the divide between our languages. In between our grammatically incorrect sentences, John Jairo would sprinkle in, "I friend. Remember."

At the time, I didn't understand why he continued to reaffirm that he was a friend. Perhaps he was genuinely friendly. Perhaps he wanted a good tip. I would later learn the basis for John Jairo's reassurance of his friendship.

John Jairo drove me beyond the mountains and through the lush forest to meet Pachamama. Known to some as Mother Earth, known to others as Gaia. In the Andes Mountains of South America, she is known as Pachamama. She is the goddess of fertility, the goddess of nature. She nourishes the Earth and protects its inhabitants. The shamans of South America concoct a potent potion to connect with Pachamama: ayahuasca.

I was on my way to my first ayahuasca ceremony to drink from the sacred vine that is believed to transport and transform the spirit. Although I sought her, John Jairo knew that Pachamama would test me. She would teach me about life, but first, she would bring me through death. John Jairo knew that I would need a friend.

I finally arrived at the *Hogar*, a small retreat protected from the bustle of Medellín by the dense forests. According to a sign above the temple, I had made it to "Donde el gran sabio medita:" where the great sage meditates. It was a simple building. Beds made of wooden planks lined the dirt floors of the outdoor temple. A small but warm fire burned in the center, and bathrooms were a short walk from the temple. The smell of sage and incense mingled with the breeze from the dense green forest that encircled the temple.

John Jairo explained that I could get up from my bed as I pleased. He instructed me to throw up in the grass outside the temple and to go to the bathrooms whenever I needed.

"You will purge. It's normal. Mind, body, spirit. Clean," John Jairo explained.

John Jairo helped me lay blankets and a pillow on my wooden bed. He then accompanied me to meet the shaman who stood solemnly at the entrance of the temple. After John Jairo translated the shaman's instructions from Spanish to English, as well as he could, the shaman handed me my first cup of ayahuasca, a brown bitter liquid. As I drank the thick tannin brew, John Jairo urged me to remember my intention. Ayahuasca is a medicine, a mirror for the mind and soul.

"Remember your intention. Remember, I friend," John Jairo said.

My intention: who am I? I am the daughter of immigrants. I am a first-generation American. I am a lawyer. But who am I, really and truly, who am I?

I saw another participant sitting on his bed. So, I sat on my bed. After a while, I watched other participants slowly lay down, and so I also lay down on my bed.

Am I supposed to be meditating? Am I supposed to be sleeping? Am I doing this right?

Unsure of what to do, I lay awake in my bed, staring at the flowers and trees surrounding the temple. I found myself enamored by a nearby tree with bright red flowers. The air felt calm, like a soothing drift drawing me into a daydream.

"I guess the medicine doesn't work on me, but at least I can enjoy the trees."

My captivation with the trees was interrupted by the shaman. The shaman asked if I was in a trance. I said no. "No colors? No sounds? No visions?" He asked in Spanish. "No," I said, despite the fact that his mouth and eyes exchanged places on his face.

John Jairo approached. "Trance? Colors? Visions?" He asked. His mouth and eyes also exchanged places, but I repeated, "No." The shaman and John Jairo asked if I wanted a second cup of ayahuasca. After politely declining, I explained to them that this was enough. I signed up for two days but only needed one day and one cup. They understood and walked away.

...

Suddenly, uncontrollable laughter filled me. Nearby, a woman sobbed, consumed by grief, but was held closely by one of the caregivers. Embarrassed by my laughter, I hid underneath my blanket. The uncontrollable laughter was then replaced by the urge to pee. I got out of bed and began the short walk to the bathroom, but as I walked, "I" was not walking. I felt that my legs were moving, one foot stepping in front of the other, but "I" was not walking. I was in a comatose state, watching myself from a third-person perspective.

I watched myself walk. I watched myself pee. It reminded me of walking my dog on her leash and watching her on our walks. But instead of the dog, I was on a leash. Who was holding my leash?

I returned to my bed with a different emotion: fear. Trying to return to my body, I touched my hair and was amazed by its softness; it felt like silk. I tried to feel my own hands. So cold. So small. Were they always this small?

I fought the medicine and tried to stay in my body. I fought the fear and panic, trying to focus on happy thoughts. "Trou," I whispered. As much as my dog, Trou, brought me love and comfort, the thought of her slipped away. Instead, I thought of my best friend, Lauren, a constant source of unconditional love throughout my life. I thought of my boyfriend, Seth, and his unwavering support and understanding. Although I was alone in the forest, thoughts of them kept me company. "Lauren. Seth. Lauren. Seth." I repeated their names as though they were the only words I knew. I yawned. I yawned again. *"Should I lay down and sleep?"* I thought as the yawns persisted. Without any instructions from my mind, my body rose from the bed.

What is it doing? Where is it going?

"Purge," it said.

I walked to the grass outside the temple, and something thick and red vomited from my body.

"Lauren. Seth. Lauren. Seth," I thought to myself. My nose began to run uncontrollably, and a caregiver approached with toilet paper. Instinctively and reflexively, my body began furiously blowing and wiping its nose.

"Lauren. Seth. Lauren. Seth," I continued in my head.

It came again. The thick red substance spewed from my body.

"Poison," it said.

Then I heard the truck: the truck that ran over my grandfather when he surrendered his life and lay down on the highway almost twenty-seven years ago to the date.

...

It was my eighth birthday. My family was visiting the Philippines for the first time since our immigration to America.

I met my mother's family in Batangas. My grandfather beamed with pride, introducing me to everyone he knew in the region. Overflowing with joy, my grandfather decided to throw me the biggest and best birthday party ever. Everyone in town was invited. I even visited a nearby sweat shop to extend the invitation to them. As immigrants in America, we had so little. We had so much to overcome and so little to celebrate. Finally, for my eighth birthday, I got to celebrate. At last, I was getting a real birthday party.

It was pure bliss. I was ecstatic on the morning of my birthday party, filled with sunshine and pure happiness. It was a dream come true, but sadly, that was the last time I would ever know that feeling.

The festivities commenced in the morning. I stood over my very own birthday cake while family and friends sang, "Maligayang bati, Maligayang bati." But then the happy birthday song in my native tongue was replaced by yelling, and by something even more native, more primitive: fear. My gaze lifted from the candles to my grandfather, who entered the room. He reached for a knife and attempted to cut his throat.

My uncle rescued him, or so I thought. His body was rescued, but his mind was lost. Throughout the day, he made several attempts to surrender. Suffocation with a plastic bag. Strangulation with the electrical cord of a VHS tape rewinder. My mother's sorrow prevailed over her wavering will to be strong. She sobbed until grief consumed her. She fainted in and out throughout the day, awakened by tears only alleviated by involuntary unconsciousness.

I knew not to cry. I wasn't allowed to cry. My parents knew that the world could be cruel, and I had to be strong. And so, they taught me not to cry. Amidst the hysteria, I attempted to trip and fall. I tripped over the rug. I tripped over the stairs. If I tripped, started bleeding and hurt myself badly enough, I would have an excuse to cry. But I was unable to cut my skin or break a bone, and so the excuse never presented itself.

In the evening, there was no sight of my grandfather. The sound of sobbing had ceased. *"Perhaps everything is okay now?"* I hoped.

Guests for my birthday party began to arrive for the evening celebration. I was in my best dress, and so I put on my very best smile.

And then it came, a knock on the door. With my very best dress and my very best smile, I answered the door, "Hi! Are you here for my party?"

A man looked down at me with sad eyes, his figure soaked with the heavy rains brought by the monsoon season.

"Can I speak to your parents?" He asked.

I watched as my parents approached. They closed the door and disappeared into the rain. I watched through the window until they finally reappeared, carrying a body. It was my grandfather.

Always being wiser than my years, I convinced myself that I knew exactly why it had happened. I didn't deserve a birthday party. I didn't deserve nice things. I was to blame for this tragedy. I was unworthy.

I had to make myself worthy.

...

"Poison," it repeated as my body continued to purge the ayahuasca from my stomach. This time, something accompanied the red sludge that spewed from my body: shame. For twenty-seven years, I had carried the burden of blaming myself for my grandfather's surrender. It took twenty-seven years, but I finally watched the poison of shame leave my body. Emilse, a healer at the ceremony, stood beside me with a shovel of sand. She covered the red sludge and with it, she buried and laid my grief to rest.

...

I felt lighter and cleaner, but still afraid. And so, I continued to fight the medicine and hold on to my body.

"Lauren. Seth. Lauren. Seth." I said to myself. John Jairo appeared. "Where is your water?" he asked. I pointed indiscernibly, and so he purchased a bottle of water.

"Drink slowly, slowly."

As I drank the water, the feeling reappeared. The purge. More poison. I fought the medicine.

"Lauren. Seth. Lauren. Seth. Lauren. Lauren. Lauren." I fought for their names. I fought for words, but Seth's name disappeared, and the very last thing I could do was scream. As loudly and with every fiber of my being, my body screamed, "LAUREN." Then the words were gone.

I was gone.

...

Caregivers approached. Fear. Panic. Rape. Rape. Rape. They're going to rape me. I'm going to die. My insides collapsed. My throat closed as I suffocated on pain.

When I was four years old, I was raped at daycare. My parents were illegal immigrants at the time, and their only possible avenue was silence. I stayed silent too.

When I was fourteen, I was raped again. My family never told me they loved me, but he did. He was the only person in the world who found me worthy of love, and so I stayed silent.

I thought I had worked past the trauma through decades of counseling, hypnotherapy, and meditation. But it clung to me still. The poison. The trauma.

The body is a vessel. A vessel for the soul, but also a vessel for something more. A vessel for every hurt, every pain, every betrayal, every disappointment, and every fear. And within my own body, the trauma, the poison was trapped. Pachamama was trying to set me free.

My body felt smothered as the terror of rape loomed over me again. "Look at me," John Jairo said.

"I friend. Friend." John Jairo continued to give me water.

"Friend," he repeated.

Instead of rape, I felt a caregiver's hand soothing me and rubbing my back. I felt another hand holding my own. Above me stood a shaman, chanting, praying, fanning away the terror, and spraying a liquid onto me that felt like hope. Finally, I purged the poison. I was free.

...

"Are you ready?" Pachamama asked.

I looked into the clouds. My body, mind and spirit answered separately but in unison, "I'm ready."

I purged until what left my body was clear and there was nothing left in my stomach to empty. But still, my body rhythmically moved and regurgitated. Instead of vomiting, I began to spit. There was still something left to purge.

I purged the anger toward my parents. I purged the anger toward my grandfather. I purged the anger toward my rapists. I purged the anger for every sour lemon and ever lousy hand of cards life had ever given me. My eyes looked up to the sky and rolled behind my eyelids as I purged. The caregivers and participants whose trances had ended observed in fear and curiosity.

"It's normal," John Jairo explained to onlookers. The healer, Emilse explained to everyone what was happening. Though I had lost the words to explain my thoughts, and my body had lost the ability to speak, Emilse, through her gifts as a healer, somehow narrated my experience to onlookers. "Forgiveness. Forgiveness for her mother. Forgiveness for her father. Forgiveness for their mothers and fathers.

Forgiveness for all of her ancestors. Forgiveness. She is doing the work of her ancestors."

...

The purging ended. Instinctively and reflexively, my body began to cry. "It's normal," John Jairo kept reciting, "It's okay to cry." The soft cry turned into sobbing, and the sobbing devolved into an unrecognizable howl into the sky. I cried tears for all the suffering I had endured, and then I cried tears that were not my own. I cried the tears that my parents were too afraid to cry, for fear that if they started crying, the crying would never end. I cried the tears of my grandparents, whose existence revolved too much on survival to truly feel grief, or anything at all.

Finally, it stopped. The purging was done. My body felt clean. After the purging, all that was left was forgiveness and love. Words came back, "Lauren. Seth."

I walked to my bed and hid underneath my blanket. Beneath the warm blanket, my body, mind, and spirit were consumed with love. And I remembered. I remembered every person who loved me. I remembered every act of kindness, every outpouring of love throughout my entire life.

...

Who am I? I am the product of my ancestors' hard work and diligence. I am the product of my parents' sacrifice, determination and unrelenting dream of a better life. I am the product of and testimony to human resilience. I am the beautiful masterpiece made by Pachamama herself. I am the love and light that family, friends, and strangers poured into me. I am only love and light.

Chapter 2
Love and Light

After I had returned to my body, I decided to stay at the retreat overnight and commit to the second day of the ayahuasca ceremony. Despite my fear, I knew that there was something more to learn from Pachamama.

As day turned to night, I sat by the fire before dinner. Grazing my feet and fingers through the sand, I found a pebble. I began scribbling in the sand, nonsensically at first, but then letters began to appear. I began to write the word "flower," but I stopped and wiped away the sand. It was the wrong word.

I began to write again. "Florence."

...

Seth and I were both world travelers. Our paths intersected when we both swiped right on a dating app. Seth's story and mine were vastly different, yet very much the same. He too was loved dearly by his parents who worked tirelessly for his future. While his parents worked long hours, he was raised by his next-door neighbor, Florence. Florence was a citizen of the world. She understood that the boundaries between nations were imaginary and that the only thing that separated humanity was a lack of understanding.

Caring for Seth through his childhood, Florence told him stories of foreign lands. She gave him the gift of understanding. After every chore Seth completed, Florence gave him a coin from a different country. Seth grew up in a small town but knew he was meant for something more. He became determined to explore the world and spend each coin from Florence. Florence was his love and light.

Florence passed away before I could meet her. In person, at least. Filled with love and light of my very own after my first ayahuasca ceremony, Florence introduced herself to me in spirit. As she shared images of her life with Seth, I spoke the word "ease." Florence then showed me the contents of Seth's heart: the ocean, calm and clear from above, but with strong currents stirring deep below that existed despite the love of friends and family. Florence's presence on this Earth was the last time that the currents within Seth had eased. Florence watched him from above in the place where things are created, "heaven," as some may call it. She could not ease the currents, but at least he was never alone.

Florence loved unconditionally without hesitation, without reservation. Florence knew that I could do the same. I could be the ease. Knowing that all was well, and all was as it should be, Florence knew that she could leave the place where things are created so that her love and light could again reincarnate into a new life on Earth.

...

I insisted that I wasn't hungry and I didn't need dinner. Emilse's stubbornness surpassed my own. She took me from my sitting-place by the fire to the dinner table, insisting that I eat and recover from my first ayahuasca ceremony.

Emilse is a healer and the widow of the shaman who created the retreat. Her husband passed away in early 2022, and she has assisted her son with running the retreat since then. Emilse is the retreat's love and light.

After finishing a salad of fresh vegetables and a warm bowl of soup, I went to the empty dormitory and rested in one of the twelve bunk beds. I was exhausted, but too afraid to sleep. However, knowing that sleep would ultimately prevail, I got ready for bed and dozed off with every light on.

An hour later, Emilse appeared by my bed with a cup of tea. She explained that she would be sleeping in the dorm in the bed across from mine to watch over me throughout the night. After ensuring that I had finished my cup of tea, she prayed for me and started walking off. But after taking a few steps, she returned to my bed and said, "Your eyes. They're so beautiful." Emilse turned off the lights before heading to bed. Although I feared the darkness, I knew I was okay. Emilse would be with me. She is love and light.

…

I woke before the sun, stretched, and tiptoed to the bathroom to avoid waking Emilse. As it was hours before the next ayahuasca ceremony, I decided to return to bed, but I couldn't sleep. Something was there. Someone was there. I turned on the flashlight of my cellphone and searched the room. I only saw Emilse. But I knew that something was there. I tried to distract myself by mindlessly scrolling through social media, hoping that whatever, whoever it was would simply leave.

Ignoring it didn't work. And so, I mustered the courage to greet the visitor. I peered into the darkness, and to my relief, it was Florence. She came to me with a question: "Are you certain?" I wasn't sure if the question was for me or for her to answer. Perhaps it was a question for us both. Florence handed me a cup of tea, motioning for me to look into the cup.

As I looked into the darkness of the tea, he was there, Seth, in the very depth, the very bottom of the darkness. I looked into his heart and saw a rope, breaking, unraveling from the tension until all that kept the rope together was a single fiber. I felt his sorrow. I felt his pain. I began to weep, slowly falling into the darkness too. Before I could fall to my knees, Florence held my arm and braced me.

"Strong. You are strong," she whispered. I brushed the darkness away from me and I knelt by Seth. I held him close to me and whispered, "There is more." The tension left the rope, and I helped Seth knot the rope together. Florence left in peace.

…

Florence left the dormitory, but someone was still there. "Please, no," my brain begged. I was afraid. I was cold. In my mind's eyes, I saw the same sand where I wrote the name "Florence."

I began to write in the sand, "Luting." It was my grandfather.

His energy, his particles were different from my own. Mine moved like a gentle breeze. His energy was frantic, scurrying in any direction that it could.

"Lolo?" I asked. There was a pause in the frantic energy and from the darkness, a response, "I'm sorry."

I tried to comfort his spirit. I explained to my Lolo that I understood and found forgiveness for the hurt he had caused me and for the hurt to my family. I told my Lolo that he could go in peace because I was okay.

"I know. I've watched you. I've always been so proud." The energy vanished. Only Emilse and I were left in the dormitory, and I found my way back to sleep.

Chapter 3
Mothers' Wisdom

The sun finally rose and so did Emilse. "The ceremony starts at 8 AM. Would you like some boiled water for a hot bath?" I nodded excitedly for a hot bath, something familiar amid my journey through the unknown. We headed to the main home's kitchen where Emilse began to boil a large pot of water.

While the water boiled, she motioned me to follow her outside. As we walked through the gardens, Emilse plucked and cut the leaves from various plants, allowing me to smell each one. The scents of eucalyptus, lemon grass, and plants that I didn't recognize filled my nose with the essence of springtime. Before taking from each plant, Emilse hovered her hand above the plant, offering a prayer of gratitude.

When we returned to the kitchen, Emilse placed the herbs into the pot of water before starting her morning routine. She prepared cups of tea, adding extra ingredients to my cup.

"Por suerte," she said, "for luck."

As I sipped my tea, I watched Emilse take various barks and plants from the pantry and place them into a bottle of water. She explained that the barks and plants were her medicine for diabetes. Emilse began to grind a vegetable I didn't recognize. It was soothing to see her make the medicine, and something about the process intrigued me.

"For cholesterol," she said.

Seeing my curiosity, Emilse took plants and vegetables out of the pantry, explaining that each one is a remedy for an ailment. A remedy from Pachamama, from Mother Earth.

As I listened to Emilse, I recalled a moment from decades before when my mother told me a story of her childhood. With little money, my mother brushed her teeth by chewing on twigs, and when anyone was injured, wounds were healed with sap from a plant. I used to laugh, and my mother chastised my childish ignorance.

"Do you know what the drugs at the pharmacy are?" My mother, a chemical engineer, asked. "They're a synthetic version of what's found in plants and nature. It's a cheap synthetic version of the real thing. The best medicine is from nature."

Watching Emilse treat her own ailments from various plants, I laughed to myself, "Mothers are always right." Pachamama gave Emilse medicine for her ailments. Perhaps Pachamama had something for me too.

After the boiling water and herbs were ready, Emilse poured the herbal water into a larger bucket, instructing me to bring it outside and fill it with the water collected from last night's rain. Before I could bring the bucket outside, Emilse walked to the pantry and returned with three jars of colored liquid, extra ingredients for the bathwater.

She poured from the first jar. "For safe travels," she said.

Then from the second jar. "For luck," she said.

Finally, from the third. "For the spirits."

After thanking Emilse, I walked through the gardens to the small outdoor washroom. As instructed, I poured fresh water from the previous night's rain into the bucket for my bath. When I poured the water onto my body, the red sludge and the residue of yesterday's purge washed away, replaced by the feeling of warmth and the smell of the forest and eternal spring. "Is it even worth it to bathe? Won't I just be filthy after the ceremony?" I thought to myself.

In response, Pachamama whispered that I should be clean. Pachamama promised that I would be even cleaner after today's ceremony.

Chapter 4
Death

Before the ayahuasca ceremony, Emilse sent me off with a hug and wished me luck. "You are strong. You will make it through your travels." Emilse's reassurances helped me conceal my nervousness as I walked assuredly to the temple.

I found the shaman and joined the group of participants, all new faces, taking Pachamama's medicine for the first time. The shaman handed me the first cup of ayahuasca. Shock spread over the faces of the new participants in disbelief at the speed I drank the bitter brew.

I found my spot in the temple, next to the fire. I watched the new participants trickling into the temple after drinking their first cup of ayahuasca. First, a man in his early twenties walked into the temple, followed by his girlfriend, who did not drink, but came to help him through his travels. "Mi Amor," he smiled at her, flashing the braces on his teeth. Then, two young men walked in together, their arms fully covered in tattoos and their faces so very unfeeling. After them came two women who entered the temple together but decided to sit outside, next to the trees. Finally, a husband and wife drank their first cups together. They entered the temple with their teenage daughter, who was there to support her parents through their journeys.

And so, we waited. We had no clocks or cellphones. Unable to know the hour, time crept forward slowly. My hand again began to scribble in the dirt as I sat by the fire and watched the wood slowly burn. The fresh log at the top of the fire began to splinter. I pulled off a small piece and used it to scribble in the sand. Emilse watched me from outside the temple.

"Escribe," she said. The scribbles turned into letters. The letters turned into words: "Align Hope Giver."

I began to trace the words. Align. Hope. Giver. Later, Emilse strolled into the temple to check on the participants. She read my words in the sand and nodded approvingly. Bored by the waiting, I continued to trace my words. Finally, I saw that the medicine was working for one of the participants. One of the young men that was covered in tattoos rose from his bed and began a lively conversation with a tree. He then walked toward the mirror in front of the bathroom and stared. He began to laugh and clap.

"Why is he clapping? What is he laughing at?" I thought. He purged the red sludge, returned to his bed laughing, and eventually fell asleep.

The young man was proof that this batch of ayahuasca worked. I was hopeful that the plant medicine would start to work for me soon. But nothing happened. There was just waiting. More waiting. I remembered what John Jairo told me before my first ceremony: remember your intention. My intention for today: what is my place in the universe?

The shaman approached. "Trance?" He asked in Spanish.

"No," I replied. He handed me a second cup of ayahuasca. I drank without hesitation, and then I waited for the universe, for Pachamama, for anyone to answer my questions.

...

More unquantifiable time passed. Then it came. My stomach churned and I felt the purge. I immediately headed to the grass outside the temple and vomited the red sludge. Oddly, nothing other than the red sludge left my body. No sadness. No spirits. Perhaps I was done purging my grief.

Caregivers wandered around the temple to care for anyone in need. I watched them as they watched me. My stomach still turned, so I stood in the grass, waiting for my next purge, prepared with my water bottle at my side.

As I stood in the grass, a little girl approached me. I assumed that she was a daughter of one of the caregivers who couldn't find a babysitter. Why was she so close to me while I was supposed to be purging out demons or sins or whatever was left inside of me?

The caregivers watched, but they didn't take the little girl away. My curiosity resigned, and I assumed she was allowed to stay because she was desensitized and would one day be a caregiver like her mother.

She was about four or five years old. Her hair was black and placed neatly behind her ears in two perfect braids. Her eyes were dark, almost black, but they glimmered with kindness and joy. She had the sweetest smile, so innocent and pure. All participants were wearing sweatshirts and were bundled in blankets, but the little girl was wearing a sundress, immune to the cold. Something about her felt surreal.

My stomach turned and I felt the purge. I squatted closer to the ground, but I refused to sit in the mud and grass. I had just taken a bath in eternal spring water, and I didn't want to ruin it.

"Purge," I said, but nothing came. The pain in my stomach grew. Desperate to purge, I knelt on the ground. The little girl knelt inches from me. She looked into my eyes and smiled. I attempted to smile back. As I looked into her face, I noticed her earrings, small gold bands with colorful cupcakes hanging from the bottom. I couldn't help but smile.

"What a perfect child," I said to myself.

Then, it finally happened. I began to purge the red sludge. I wiped my face and searched for the girl, hoping she hadn't seen me, hoping she had looked away. Instead, I saw her, on her knees, mimicking my gestures and pretending to vomit. Saddened, I quickly picked myself up and stood.

I heard Pachamama's voice, "She will watch you. You are her teacher. Be careful of what you teach her."

The pain in my stomach grew. I felt my mind losing control of my body. But I smiled and stood firm because the little girl was watching me. My eyes met her eyes, her perfect little eyes. She smiled and began to run with her arms extended like an airplane. I laughed. She laughed harder.

She ran back to me, asking if we could play in my room. I told her no, but maybe later. She continued to smile and sat patiently next to me.

I needed to purge. My body needed to fall. But I didn't. I wouldn't. She was watching me constantly. So instead, I returned to my bed and lay underneath my blanket. The little girl followed me, still wishing, still hoping that I would play.

Pachamama laughed. "This is kids. You never get a break." I laughed with Pachamama.

No breaks. And so, I sat up. The little girl smiled even more brightly. I hadn't realized how much sunshine one face could hold. She was brighter than the sun. The little girl noticed that my shoes were untied, and she attempted to tie my shoes. She made "bunny ears" with the laces.

I laughed to myself. The bunny ears reminded me of the bunny ears my cousin, Norcelene made when she taught me how to tie my shoes. I tied my right shoe while the little girl stumbled and fumbled with the left. Finally, she looked up at me, and I took the laces from her. I slowly tied the laces. Her eyes grew bigger with curiosity, carefully watching each step.

"She is such a caring, smart and curious child," I thought to myself. My mind was slowly separating and losing control over my body, but my body still managed to smile.

After tying both shoes, the little girl noticed that my fingernails were painted five different colors of purple and sprinkled with glitter. She laughed and examined each finger. I felt her small gentle fingers touch mine and wondered at how small her hands were. Her hands left mine and reached for her face. She began making faces with her hands, and I laughed.

The little girl gestured toward her eyes. She was pointing at her eyes, but I couldn't understand her. She used her small fingers to make her eyes bigger and smaller. She stopped, and we stared at each other for a while. We had the exact same eyes.

Her fingers moved towards her lips, and she smiled. I knew that smile. She had Seth's smile. Then, she spoke.

"Florence Lauren."

She moved my water bottle closer to my hand, waved goodbye sweetly, and skipped into the forest. I finally connected the dots. Florence Lauren. I had just met Florence Lauren: my future daughter that was yet to exist.

...

I lay in my bed, panicking as I realized that I was hallucinating. I needed to purge the plant medicine. I didn't have a daughter. Florence Lauren wasn't real. What is real? Is Emilse real? Is Seth real? Had I made him up?

"Nothing is real," said my mind. At that moment, I knew nothing but panic. I rushed to the grass as quickly as my body would allow, and I attempted to purge. I drank more water in hopes that it would clean my stomach of the plant medicine. Water. More water. Need water. Need...

My words left me.

...

I watched two of the female caregivers walking happily towards the bathroom. One of the caregivers started to unzip her pants before she made it to the bathroom. I saw her enter a stall. She left the door open and looked at me. She was pooping. At least I think she was pooping.

...

I struggled to purge, but the red sludge didn't come. I was no longer in a comfortable human shape. I was crouching like an animal, my nails digging into the ground like claws.

The two female caregivers walked slowly towards me. I stared at them, unable to speak. I continued to stare, hoping that they would understand that I needed help. A caregiver handed me toilet paper. But she realized that I was not staring at the roll of toilet paper. I was staring at her hand. Without instruction, my body reflexively reached for her hand and squeezed. Her hand squeezed back. She knelt beside me to hold my hand. The second caregiver did the same.

I lost my breath. I couldn't breathe. There was no air, and the world started to fade. The caregivers rubbed my back, held my drooping head up and encouraged me to breathe. My body began to breathe, but it sounded more animal than human. I no longer recognized my body. From a distance, my mind and spirit were watching a dying animal fighting for its last breaths.

The two caregivers attempted to carry me to my bed. The shaman came to help. As I lay in my bed, my grip around the hands of the caregivers tightened. The shaman stood above me, beginning his prayers, fanning away death and spraying me with hope. The caregiver holding my left hand grabbed my face.

"Look at me," she said. She breathed slowly and rhythmically, and my body copied hers. My breaths became more human. As my mind and spirit watched my body from a distance, I was reminded of movies and television shows I had watched of women, women giving birth.

Without instruction, my body crawled toward the bathroom. The shaman and the caregivers lifted me. Instead of politely squatting over the public toilet, I sat on the toilet seat the second my pants fell. I screamed. I pushed. No air. There was no air.

"Breathe," the shaman told me. He was fanning behind the stall door, spraying hope onto me from above the door. The shaman continued his prayers. I screamed. I pushed. I started to breathe. I was in labor. I was giving birth to the little girl that I had hallucinated moments before, Florence Lauren.

...

My body stopped pushing. My arms clumsily shoved the stall door open, and my body collapsed into the shaman's arms. The shaman and caregivers carried me to my bed. My body laid still and weak, but my hand remained clenched tightly around a caregiver's wrist. No air. She was my only connection to life.

As I lay in bed, another caregiver held my face. "Watch me. Watch me," she said, praying that I would breathe again. There was no breath. No human life. Only the breaths of a dying animal. Emilse rushed to my side. She reached for my right hand, which instinctively reached for her knee, slowly creeping to her shoulder.

Hug. Alone. Hold. Dark. Cold.

My body reached for Emilse, but she gently laid my head back onto the bed. Whatever energy remained, my body used it to scream and sob instead of breathing. Emilse began to pray. The shaman furiously fanned away death as Emilse sang the song of Pachamama. Her song ended, and she asked:

"Do you forgive your mother?" Without instruction, my head nodded.

"Do you forgive your father?" It nodded again.

"Do you forgive all who have hurt you?" It nodded.

"Do you forgive your God?" It nodded.

"Do you forgive yourself?"

Emilse repeated her question. "Do you forgive yourself?" No nod. No answers. My hand started to unclench. With my last ounce of strength, I reached for Emilse. She lifted and held my body.

Hug. Alone. Hold. Dark. Cold.

Emilse held my body as a caregiver held my head. "Look at me. Repeat after me," the caregiver instructed. I wanted to repeat, but I couldn't hear her words. Her voice faded. I surrendered. My body died in Emilse's arms.

Chapter 5
Rebirth

I could not bring life back to this world. Despite the purge, there was still poison trapped inside my vessel. My vessel was still unclean, still unworthy. The poison trapped within me surged, searching for an escape.

This body earned a bachelor's degree in three years, with a 4.0 GPA, while working two jobs. Still unworthy. Still unclean.

This body fulfilled her childhood dream of becoming a lawyer at age twenty-three. Still unworthy. Still unclean.

This body completed triathlons and marathons. Still unworthy. Still unclean.

Jiu Jitsu. Muay Thai. Aerial acrobatics. Still unworthy. Still unclean.

Transformed from a poor child to a world-traveling lawyer. Still unworthy. Still unclean.

Evolved from being an illegal immigrant living in a one-bedroom apartment with her family into a self-sufficient homeowner. Still unworthy. Still unclean.

Training to hike Everest and run a marathon in Greece after recovering from life-threatening illnesses, injuries, surgeries, and seven hospitalizations. Still unworthy. Still unclean.

Still unworthy. Still unclean. Still unworthy. Still unclean. Still unworthy. Still unclean.

My body and my mind spiraled until finally, I stood in utter darkness.

Then, through the darkness, my soul whispered, "Worthy. Born worthy. Created worthy."

But I had persecuted and abused my body. I had punished myself by starving and purging as a teenager, to be thin, to be worthy. I cut into my skin when worthiness was still out of reach. I forced my body to compete, to perform, to endure when it simply needed rest. An enemy to myself, I battled my own body and declared a seemingly endless war against myself.

But my soul whispered, "Worthy. Always worthy."

Then, through the darkness, my mind spoke, "No Everest. No marathon. Rest."

Another voice, speaking even louder, interrupted the conversation. Pachamama spoke through the darkness, words similar to the words of John Jairo when we first met on our drive to the retreat. "Friends. ¿Entiende? You understand?"

Body, mind and soul: they were friends. They were finally at peace. I answered, "Sí."

…

Slowly I returned. Returned to Emilse. She sprayed a brown elixir over my body and rubbed a green balm on my forehead where my third eye resided. As I returned, I heard the shaman whistle and sing the songs of Pachamama. Caregivers kneeled at both sides. My right hand was held by a man. My vision was slowly returning. I saw his mouth whispering prayers underneath tears, with flashes of his braces in between his words. He had already endured the ayahuasca and traveled on his journey with Pachamama. Now he was helping me with mine. I held his hand tightly. Instinctively, my index and middle finger released, only to crawl underneath the golden chain around his wrist and lay above his pulse.

As my senses returned, his girlfriend whispered above me, "You're okay. You're okay." The other participants of the ceremony had finished their journeys and were circled around me. Crying. Praying. Carrying me through the rest of my journey with their newfound strength.

Emilse asked again, "Do you forgive yourself?"

This time I answered aloud, "Sí."

"Do you forgive everything?"

"Sí."

"She is ready," Emilse said to the caregiver next to me. The caregiver held my head in her hands. I looked into her eyes. Kind like mine. "Repeat after me."

I nodded.

"I forgive it all," she said. My words returned, and I repeated.

"I forget it all," the caregiver said.

I began to sob, but I tried to repeat, "I forget…" My words were interrupted by sobs. I struggled, but I finally uttered, "I forget…I forget it all. All. I forget it all."

The caregiver lowered my head and I sobbed into my bed. Emilse soothed me. "Well done. Your mission is complete. You can rest. Your mission is complete. There is no past. Only now. Only the future. Your mission is complete. It's time to rest."

The past faded. I forgot. I forgot it all.

...

Emilse pressed her thumb over my third eye, with the rest of her fingers lightly over my eyelids, encouraging me to sleep. My eyes stayed open, and I continued to cry softly.

"Think of the future. Think of your love," Emilse said.

"Was Florence Lauren real? Is Seth real? Is anything real?" I thought to myself as I cried.

As if she heard my every thought, Emilse continued, "Think of your future. Your lover. Your love. Love is real. Rest. See your love. See your future."

Emilse again encouraged my eyes to rest as she pressed over my third eye with her thumb. She encouraged me to sleep, but my eyes remained open. Even with my eyes open, I could see. I saw into the beyond. Even before taking Pachamama's medicine, I could always see into the beyond. But with the help of Pachamama and Emilse, my sight had sharpened. Further, clearer, I could see effortlessly and infinitely into the beyond.

...

Breathe. Just breathe. I continued to push, allowing each breath to push through the pain. I envisioned the hand that I was holding was actually Seth's. It was his body holding mine, and not the body of Emilse. Visions of Seth's journeys. Visions of mine. Lessons we had learned, the wisdom we had earned that allowed us to meet in this space and time. Visions of a face: Florence Lauren's face, with my eyes and his smile. A culmination of our hard-earned peace. A beautiful child that carried no sin from her ancestors. A gift of heaven's grace perfected.

...

I stared into the trees next to the temple. Visions of Florence Lauren appeared. Her laughter. Her joy. Her father. Visions of the possibilities of our future in this life appeared. Visions of our lives to come followed.

Seth. Cancer. Visions of despair, followed by visions of hope. He lives. He endures. He endures for Florence Lauren. He endures for us.

Visions continued to a future I didn't believe could ever exist. Learning as a child that surrender was an option and suicide was an escape, I automatically assumed that I too would surrender. But the universe unfolded and showed me otherwise.

Visions of Seth. With grayer hair, but the same, kind smile. His mind fades, memories come and go. But he looks into my eyes, and he comes back. Time passes, and his mind drifts further and further. His last and only memory is the face of Florence Lauren laughing at his attempts to make balloon animals. His eyes see her eyes. He remembers my eyes. He drifts into death, but he remembers to search for my eyes and find me in the life to come.

Chapter 6
Masters

My body still lay in the temple. My mind and spirit returned little by little. I felt the gold chain of the man holding my hand. I felt his pulse. The gentle beat of his life. Reflexively, my other hand reached up, touching his chest, searching for his heart. His emotions flowed into my body. I saw the grief that brought him to take Pachamama's medicine. I saw into the beyond and the visions of his purpose in this life. I spoke to him and shared a message from beyond. A message I could no longer remember. It wasn't for me to remember. His girlfriend stood behind us, translating from English to Spanish. He cried. He understood the message. His tears were followed by a soft uttering, "Gracias."

Searching the temple, I saw the two young men covered in tattoos. They had entered the ceremony with emotionless faces and cold demeanors. But next to me, they sat smiling. They were too far to reach, but I envisioned one hand on their wrists, another on their hearts. I saw the source of their anger and its dissipation into acceptance with the help of Pachamama.

I felt their emotions. I felt it all. My hands lowered to the ground and my nails clawed into the dirt beside me. Bodies are vessels, absorbing far more than we know and containing far more than we realize. But as I looked into their hearts, and their emotions flowed through my veins, my body did not serve as a vessel for their sorrows. As my hands still clawed into the earth, their sorrows flowed through me and into Pachamama for her to recycle, to transform.

My body, still worthy, still clean, now looked into the faces of the people that surrounded me. I saw beyond their suffering. I saw their purposes and their missions in life. Inside every person, I saw God.

...

Visions and messages appeared from the trees, from the flowers, from the vines, and from the birds. I began to connect the dots. Every moment, every heartbreak, every joy made sense. It served my mission. My purpose. Staring into the beyond, I spoke, "Forgiveness." My purpose in this life is forgiveness. The universe had gifted me with the hardest transgressions and trespasses against my body, mind and soul, offering me the lesson of forgiveness. I accepted.

My visions drifted to the people I love, visions of their light and their life purposes. We were Masters in this life and the lives to come.

In every life, there is a lesson. A purpose. Lives continue past the doorway of death. Lessons continue until learned. With each lesson completed, we earn wisdom about what it means to live, fly, and be free. Once every lesson is learned, we complete our mission. We find liberation.

In the temple where the great sage meditates, I completed my mission. Through the purge, through the red sludge, I had pushed forward and discovered liberation. I was finally free.

...

My visions returned to a memory, a week before my trip to Colombia. I was sitting on the couch crying. Seth listened.

"I try. I try really hard. I give so much to so many people. I don't understand how I keep pouring so much into people who care so little." I wished for a new heart. A heart that cared less, gave less. Seth waited for me to finish before he spoke.

"I know exactly how you feel."

"Then how do you do it? How do you make it hurt less?"

"I found someone who knows exactly how I feel."

...

Through the clouds, I saw visions from far beyond. Visions of the place where things are created. Seth, Florence Lauren and I appear, but this time as butterflies. Through space and time, we fly, reuniting in lives to come. Learning, teaching, giving, and spreading our light so that others may find the path to liberation.

In the place where things are made, we meet. Countless Masters. From time to time, our lives intersect. From time to time, they don't. But we eventually return to the place where things are created. Reuniting. We embrace. We fill each other with love and light before returning to a new life, to share our lights with those still voyaging to liberation. To help the souls seeking liberation, we spread our light so that they may discover themselves from the darkness.

Chapter 7
The Comedian

I heard a joke once: if you want to make God laugh, tell him your plans.

...

I continued to stare into the beyond. Visions appeared of the Botero statues Lauren and I had seen days before in Medellín, statues of Adam and Eve. Messages followed, explanations of the beauty and the perfection of humanity, despite the lessons we have yet to learn. Gratitude for my journey overflowed. Gratitude for this life, this journey here on Earth. Gratitude for my body, perhaps my favorite vessel and home so far, as I journey back and forth from the place where things are created.

Visions appeared of the Phoenix statue Lauren and I had passed on our day trip to Guatape. Rebirth through fire. I recalled with gratitude every moment and every detail of this life which led to my rebirth in the temple where the great sage meditates.

I started to laugh. Remembering the things that once caused suffering, I laughed. It all made sense. Then, I heard a voice. A new voice. A voice just as powerful as that of Pachamama. The voice of the ultimate creator. The voice of God.

…

He grinned and winked, in the way that universal formless energies grin and wink.

"What do you think?" He asked.

"Well done, well done."

He bowed as I graciously clapped for his masterpiece. I thought of how, in my twenties, I used to go to comedy shows and watch some of the funniest comedians. But this show, God's masterpiece, was the funniest show of them all. I laughed as I continued to clap.

Chapter 8
Align Hope Giver

My body, mind and soul reunited and embraced. I had finally completed my journey with Pachamama. I sat up from my bed. It had been nine hours since the start of my journey with today's fellow participants and travelers. The entire temple was now empty. The other travelers had finished their journeys hours before.

John Jairo appeared and sat next to me. With my breathing now human, but still labored, John Jairo held my hand and helped me to breathe. As I held his hand, I felt his pulse. Tears fell from my eyes as his emotions passed from his veins through mine.

"You friend. I friend," he said.

"Sí," I responded.

With intention and purpose, my other hand reached towards his chest and found his heart. His emotions flowed through my veins, and visions of his life appeared. He had no wife. No family. No friends other than the people he interacted with at the retreat. I explained to John Jairo the source of my tears.

"Your family is not good to you. I understand. I understand. I am your friend. You are strong, but it is okay to cry. I cried, and you can cry too."

His eyes watered, but no tears followed. "You, in my heart. But me, you forget," said John Jairo.

"John Jairo, I will remember you. I will remember my friend, John Jairo. ¿Entiende? You understand?"

He fought his tears and responded, "Sí."

…

John Jairo helped me with my bags as I thanked the shaman, the caregivers and Emilse. The shaman performed a final ritual. I sat with my back toward him as he sang thanks to Pachamama and did a final fanning and spraying of hope.

Although we had already said our goodbyes, Emilse insisted on walking me to the car for a final farewell. Before opening the car door, she held me for the last time. "Well done. You travelled well with love." She kissed both of my cheeks farewell and began her walk back to the retreat, but after a few steps, she returned to me and said a prayer. She gave me a blessing that I didn't comprehend. She finished and explained, "A blessing for a baby."

…

The next day, I returned to the airport in Medellín. It was August 15, 2022. My thirty-fifth birthday. I was exhausted but grateful to make my way home. Light. Clean. Free. Certain of my purpose. I had found forgiveness and freedom. It is my purpose to help others do the same.

I sifted through the airport. A man bumped into me, and I braced myself before I could trip. He moved on without a glance, without an apology. Another man yelled at a helpless airport employee about the long lines. A woman rushed to the airport gate, dropping her trash on the ground without hesitation. Another woman pushed and prodded her crying toddler through the airport without compassion for his discomfort in an unfamiliar and chaotic environment.

As I waited in line to board my flight home, I stopped. I looked. I felt. Many persons with many lessons yet to learn, some more than others. Many persons with many hurts needing healing, some deeper than others.

I was still uncertain of my exact path, but hopeful to help, hopeful to heal. Without financial means, without influence, without power, how could I possibly help the world, my brothers, my sisters, my fellow travelers to liberation? I breathed. I breathed the breath that carried me through my journey with ayahuasca, through death and towards life. Finally, an answer. Not from Pachamama. Not from God.

The answer came from the God existing in my own vessel, within my own beautiful body. She answered: "You are strong, armored with the kindest of hearts. Your strength. Your stories. Your kindness. They will shake the world."

Chapter 9

Integration

Two flights and eight hours later, I finally made it home to Saint Petersburg, Florida. Weary from my travels, I dove quickly into bed and swiftly fell asleep. I hoped to hibernate, to fall into a deep slumber and rise rejuvenated and prepared to take on the world with my newfound insight and understanding of the universe.

But just as rapidly as I had fallen asleep, I jolted out of bed. It was a few minutes after 3 AM. My heart raced, my body trembled, and I was laboring to breathe, just as I did during the ayahuasca ceremony. Although we were over a thousand miles apart, I somehow heard Emilse, her soothing voice was striving to calm me.

"Just breathe," Emilse said gently.

I was alone in my bedroom, but somehow, I began to hear the voice of the shaman singing the songs of Pachamama.

I panicked. I struggled to breathe as my hands grew numb. A coldness started to consume me. The ayahuasca was out of my system. Why was I hearing voices? Hearing songs? Filled with fear that perhaps I was having a negative reaction to the ayahuasca, I frantically drove to the emergency room of a nearby hospital.

"Aya what?" The nurse asked. "You did what in the forest?" The nurse questioned.

I did my best to explain the plant medicine of Pachamama as the nurse did his best to hide his judgment. I cried quietly as he finished typing his notes. "Okay, the doctor will be right in," the nurse said as he made his way out of the room. Frightened that I was still hearing the voices of Emilse and the shaman over a thousand miles away, I made sure to keep the door open as the nurse left the room.

Stifling my sobs, I waited patiently for the doctor. Emilse's voice was still in my head, striving to reassure me that all was well. Finally, her voice was interrupted by the voice of a man behind the emergency room door.

"Who's in the next room? Is it the ayahuasca chick?" The doctor asked the attending nurse. They shared a chuckle, wiped the disdain from their faces, and entered the room.

Based on the nurse's notes, a few minutes of conversation, and even fewer minutes of eye contact, the doctor concluded that I was perfectly well and was simply having a panic attack. Nonetheless, the doctor recommended medical treatment: an antipsychotic injection typically given to stabilize patients with schizophrenia and a prescription for anxiety medication.

"Forgive me, but if I'm just having a panic attack, why do I need medication?"

Annoyed by my inquiry, the doctor explained the benefits of each drug. I remained unsure and unconvinced. "Well, do you want my help or not?" The doctor asked sharply.

We eventually compromised: I took the prescription for anxiety medication and drove to the twenty-four-hour pharmacy.

Still a few hours before sunrise, the streets were completely empty as I drove to the pharmacy. Alone in my car, I sobbed. The fear from my panic attack was replaced by something new: anger. Anger towards my grandfather, my rapists, and my parents.

The anger was quickly accompanied by sorrow. I drove faster to the pharmacy, rushing and hoping for relief. But as I drove, Emilse's voice in my head grew louder and clearer, "Do not bury. Do not bury what you have unburied. Purge," she said gently.

I trusted Emilse during the ayahuasca ceremony, and I trusted her still. I crumpled the prescription, changed my course, and made my way home. As I drove home, I sobbed. I screamed. My screams became words. My words became sentences. My sentences became poetry.

> I will not carry the weight of your sin.
> It is yours to carry, and not my own.
> When my innocent eyes looked to you,
> You took your life, and I slowly lost my own.
> But that is your sin to carry, and your sin alone.
>
> I will not carry the weight of your sin.
> It is yours to carry, and not my own.
> You taught me that life was worthless,
> Something that easily comes and goes.
> But that is your sin to carry, and your sin alone.
>
> You trespassed on my innocence, the pureness of my soul.
> But that is your sin to carry, and your sin alone.
>
> I will not carry the weight of your sin.
> It is yours to carry, and not my own.
> You told me to be silent. You told me to be still.
> But something inside me rotted; something inside me grew cold.
> But that is your sin to carry, and your sin alone.

> I will not carry the weight of your sin.
> It is yours to carry, and not my own.
> You violated my body, using it for the needs of your own.
> But that is your sin to carry, and your sin alone.
>
> I will not carry the weight of your sin.
> It is yours to carry, and not my own.
> The weight I've tried to shed.
> The weight I've tried to purge.
> Deceived into believing it should be shed from my body, the vessel for my soul.
> But the weight that should be lost is that of your original sin, your sin, and yours alone.
>
> I will not carry the weight of your sin.
> It is not mine to carry.
> It is yours and yours alone.

I purged, transforming sobs and sorrow into a soliloquy and anger into art.

The next day, the only voice I heard in my head was my own. Though the sounds of Emilse's comforting voice and the songs of Pachamama faded, their love and light endured.

...

Weeks later, Pachamama's medicine was no longer coursing through my body. There was no trace of the red sludge in my stomach. But still, I needed to purge. To purge traces of past poison. To purge the struggles and stresses of each new day, preventing them from festering. Some days, I purged in the form of tears. Most days, I purged by walking away from the things that no longer served me and walking towards the path of my highest good.

I abandoned the hustle and rejected the grind that encapsulated my former, over-stressed and over-stimulated lifestyle. I slowed my body with yoga. I stilled my mind with music and painting. I soothed my soul with meditation. I strengthened the harmony between my body, mind and soul with energy healing.

I stopped eating meat. An animal knowing only captivity and abuse, carries in its being the poisons of fear and suffering: poisons that I could no longer stomach. Instead, I filled my plate with fruits and vegetables, rooted in the soil and sustained directly by Pachamama herself.

The comforting voice of Emilse that once resided in my head was replaced by my own guiding voice. Each day I honored it. Each day I grew stronger. My chronic illnesses, uncurable by doctors, had vanished. My allergies dissipated. I started and ended each day with meditation and gratitude instead of a handful of medications. My body knew exactly how to heal itself. After decades of relying on doctors who medicated my symptoms, I learned to trust my body, and it finally found the cure.

Chapter 10
The Protector of Mankind

Pachamama kept her promise. She brought me through the death of my old ways and towards a life with more meaning and purpose. But still, something inside me wanted. Hungered. Searched. Throughout my life, I have carried a need for something that I could not articulate. I searched the world endlessly for an antidote or answer.

I bathed in the sacred Ganges River and learned life's secrets from gurus in India. I sought wisdom from shamans in the Andes Mountains of South America. I chanted with monks throughout Asia. I walked in the shoes of tribes in the valleys of Kenya, Berbers in the mountains of Morocco, and Bedouins in the deserts of Jordan. I camped beneath the Northern Lights in the Arctic. I dove into the depths of the oceans and seas. I sought insight from the Wonders of the World and the pyramids and temples of Egypt. My sojourn called me to partake in ayahuasca in the evergreen forests of Colombia. But something inside me still hungered, still searched.

As I sat in my living room, sipping on my evening tea, I stared through the window, still searching for answers. What country was next on my list of travels? What sacred and ancient wisdom had I yet to call upon? What stone had I yet to turn? My rumination was interrupted as I spotted a dog outside my window, pacing in the street.

I went out to investigate more closely. Across the street from my quiet, comfortable home, my neighbor's yard was littered with garbage and old clothes. Among the strewn rubbish was my neighbor's dog, Thor, named after the Norse god of thunder and the sky: the protector of mankind. But the Thor that stood before me appeared to be the one in need of protection. His fur was covered with dirt and spurs. His nails were so overgrown that it altered his gait. Thor's gaunt body displayed each rib, expanding and contracting with each weary breath.

My knocks on my neighbor's door went unanswered. I peered through the window, and the house was empty. My neighbor was gone. She had taken her furniture, her clothes, and her belongings. All that was left was the trash in the yard and Thor.

For hours, I tried to lure Thor out of his yard and into my house. Despite my offerings of food and toys, Thor remained fearful. As the sun set, Thor planted himself on the outdoor patio he knew as home. It reeked from the stench of urine and garbage, mingled with the humidity of the Florida summer. As John Jairo had done in Colombia, I reassured Thor that I was a friend trying to help. As Emilse had done during my ayahuasca ceremony, I strived to comfort Thor. But still, Thor growled and retreated to the corner of the patio. That evening, Thor slept on the grimy patio floor, surrounded by the paint chips from the deteriorating walls and floors.

My continued efforts to befriend Thor prevailed in the morning. After a bowl of breakfast kibble, a bag of treats, and a few squeaky toys, Thor welcomed my hand as I petted his head and scratched behind his ears. He shadowed my every step, wagging his tail as he followed. After earning Thor's trust, I carried him into my car and drove to a nearby animal shelter.

Thor trembled during the drive, and his fear and distrust reappeared when the workers at the animal shelter dragged him by his leash from the car to the shelter. He dug his paws into the earth, resisting the pulls on his leash. His efforts were overpowered by the two workers dragging him, but that did not stop Thor from wailing and growling. Once we had made it into the shelter, Thor cowered and trembled in the corner of the cold room where he would be evaluated.

The lack of compassion shown to Thor at the animal shelter reminded me of my post-ayahuasca visit to the emergency room. In the same hurried fashion as the emergency room doctor, the worker at the animal shelter hastily completed the evaluation and concluded that Thor was unfit for adoption: he was deemed aggressive, and the only solution was euthanasia.

The animal shelter was wrong about Thor. His fear was misinterpreted as aggression. His deprivation of nurturing and compassion from his prior owner was erroneously construed as grounds for euthanasia: unworthy of a new home, unworthy of life. I refused to surrender him to the animal shelter. With Thor following closely behind me, I left the animal shelter, determined to prove that he was worthy of a new life and a forever home.

The following day, Thor blossomed. Showered with treats, toys and love, Thor learned to trust. He learned to love. The fearful dog that once growled and retreated from my touch now greeted me with kisses and a wagging tail. I knew that Thor was ready to find his forever home. We drove to a different animal shelter, and though he was hesitant, Thor walked happily into the animal shelter lobby. With his irresistible energy and sweet demeanor, the animal shelter welcomed Thor and assured me that they would labor tirelessly until they found Thor his forever home.

Thor and I said our goodbyes, exchanging our final kisses. Before we parted ways, I could have sworn that Thor winked: the same way God had winked in the forest of Colombia when he revealed that he was the comedian masterfully orchestrating life.

It was then that I connected the dots. All that Thor needed to save him from his circumstances was love and light: to be reminded that his loving nature still existed behind his fear. To be reminded that there was still goodness and light in the world.

I recalled the Medicine Woman's Prayer: "For you are not broken, I will not heal you, for I see you in your wholeness. I will walk with you through the darkness, as you remember your light."

I finally understood. After years of scouring the world, searching in the heights of the mountains and the depths of the oceans, I knew the exact location where I could pacify my endless, aching need. I knew the exact destination for my next trip. I knew the exact source of the wisdom I had yet to call up. It was time to turn the final stone.

Chapter 11
As Above, So Below

My house in Saint Petersburg, Florida was simple: a quaint, light blue house with a small herb garden inspired by the garden in Colombia where Emilse picked her herbs. A cozy room in the front of the house faced eastward, welcoming the rays from every sunrise. In the room warmed by sunrise, I created my "zen den." A large jute rug woven into the shape of the sun adorned the floor. Vibrant green plants in white pots lined the walls. On the floor, surrounded by plants of varying shapes and sizes, was a tan cushion seat without legs. It was in this seat that I meditated each day. It was in this seat that I would be transported to my next destination.

I burned white sage, cleansing the space in the same way that the shaman in Colombia cleansed the temple for the ayahuasca ceremony. I burned a stick of palo santo: the holy wood of the saints. The burning palo santo filled the room with its rich, wooden fragrance, reminding me of the small fire that burned at the center of the temple where I first met Pachamama.

I took a seat on the cushion, admiring the broad green leaves of the potted plants beside me before I closed my eyes. With my legs folded and my hands gently resting in my lap, my body found stillness. My mind found stillness shortly thereafter.

In the stillness, my spirit began to levitate and hover above my body. Then slowly, my spirit continued to float above my light blue house, above the trees, above the coast of the ocean. Further and further, my spirit floated, traveling through space and time. Finally, it slowly descended to its intended destination: my grandfather's home in the town of Batangas, Philippines on August 15, 1995: the day of my eighth birthday party.

My spirit drifted through the house until she finally found the person she was searching for: myself. A sad, lonely little girl on the day of her eighth birthday. She wore a white dress covered in pink flowers and green leaves. Flowers were woven into her neatly combed hair. In her best dress, the little girl sat on the floor, staring at the cord of the VHS tape rewinder. Just moments before, it was wrapped around her grandfather's neck as he attempted to strangle himself and end his life.

Like the waves of an ocean during a storm, sorrow and confusion bombarded my spirit as she moved closer to the little girl. But through it all, the little girl remained silent and still. Not a single tear was to be found on her stoic face. My spirit sat beside the little girl, extended her arms, and embraced the little girl tightly. The emotions coursing through the little girl flowed into my spirit: fear, confusion, sadness, shame. The little girl's feelings traveled into my spirit, traversed through space and time, and into my present-day body meditating in the den. In the quaint, light-blue Florida house, separated from the little girl by thousands of miles and twenty-seven years, my present-day body wept every tear that the little girl was too afraid to cry. My present-day body wailed, purging the fear, confusion, and shame that traveled through space and time from the eight-year-old girl I once was.

Still in the small house in Batangas, my spirit released her embrace around the little girl. My spirit hovered her hands over the little girl's head above her crown chakra: the bridge to the divine. My spirit filled the little girl with the gift of knowing that she was connected to something greater than any grief: she was connected to the divine.

The hands of my spirit then moved to the center of the little girl's head, hovering above her third eye and granting her the gift of sight: a discerning intuition that could see beyond any veil and find the goodness in the universe, the godliness in all people and the divinity in all things.

My spirit moved its hands, hovering above the little girl's throat, granting her the gift of expression and the promise that she would one day be liberated and free to speak her truth.

The hands of my spirit then hovered about the little girl's heart, granting her the gift of compassion and empathy: for those that loved her, for those that would harm her, and most importantly, for herself.

Continuing her mission to spread love and light, my spirit moved her hands lower, hovering above the little girl's solar plexus. My spirit filled the little girl with the gift of fire, a fire that would burn within her and glow throughout her. The fire would light her way, always guiding her through the darkness.

The hands of my spirit hovered just below the little girl's naval, over her sacral chakra. My spirit gave the little girl the gift of creation. Despite her acquaintance with poverty, hardship, and trauma at such a young age, the little girl held within her the ability to create a life of abundance and joy.

My spirit moved its hands lower, hovering above the little girl's root chakra at the base of her spine. From there, my spirit shared with the little girl the feeling of hiking through mountains, traveling across deserts, diving into the depths of the oceans, and traversing through jungles. My spirit granted the little girl the gift of finding comfort and security in any place and every space. My spirit gifted the little girl the promise that she would always find her bearings and she would always find the way despite the fallibility of people and uncertainty of the future.

In a final effort to fill the little girl with love and light, my spirit began to blow air from its lips, recreating the air generated by the shaman's fanning above my body during the ayahuasca ceremony. Love and light encapsulated the little girl. As though witnessing the moment of creation itself, my spirit watched the image of the little girl slowly disintegrate into small particles of light. The particles gracefully swayed until they transformed into thousands of colorful butterflies.

The butterflies floated through the heavens, surrounded by a mist. My spirit peered into the mist, attempting to examine its particles. The multitude of molecules were not mere particles. They were the countless prayers of my mother and father. Prayers that their God grant me safe passage through a world that they were still trying to navigate. Prayers for strength knowing that they could not shield me from every hardship.

Through space and time, the butterflies fluttered with the mist, weaving through the timeline of my life. Finding every fracture, every instance of suffering, there, the mist would travel, and a butterfly would land, as a promise of hope, as a reminder of my love and light.

The butterflies continued to flutter, to years my body had yet to know and places I had yet to go. But as my soul had completed its mission, it parted ways with the kaleidoscope of butterflies and slowly made its way back to my body, still meditating in the den of the quaint, light-blue Florida house.

As my soul reunited with my body, the fire within the center of my being ignited, blazing brighter than ever before. I embraced the journey of my life. I had finally quieted the endless searching.

Through the plant medicine of ayahuasca, I spoke to Pachamama and learned to honor the Earth and its abundance. I laughed with the Ultimate Creator and learned to humble myself to the infinite potential of the universe. And now, I unleashed the God dwelling within myself and learned of my limitless power to wield love and light.

Despite every trial and tribulation on my journey, I am worthy. Beyond worthy.

I am divine.

Made in the USA
Middletown, DE
20 December 2024

67797949R00033